MW01228580

"Feeling Different"

...the struggle navigating who you were, who you have become and who you've always been.

By: Sade' Jay

ACKNOWLEDGEMENTS

ALL praise due to God for life and a destiny that was designed purposefully, before I ever entered earth's realm.

To my mother, you knew something I didn't understand. Your life was worth all my time. Grateful to be a part of your legacy.

Special thanks to Shani! May we never forget anyone that will put their hand to the plow and look back is not fit for the kingdom. Cultivating for the culture!

THANK YOU

PREFACE

If I have never been certain of

anything in this life; I'm certain that

God is REAL, and we are

accountable for what we know!!

I've been feeling different lately…

I'm sure there are many reasons

why…

It's important that I figure it out…

I never want to live a lie!

<u>CHAPTER 1</u>

Why now…

It's always easier to ask a question than it is to answer it. I suppose the simplest answer to me is sort of complicated to articulate completely. It's like some days I'm all in. I'm all for the life that I am living. Other days, it is my job that's not fulfilling me. Meanwhile, on the next day it's my love life. If it's neither of these things, then perhaps it's my friendships or not having enough family around.

Sometimes I think I need a hobby or something. When all those things are perfectly proportioned and balanced in my life, I know what is "off" …its ME!!

Of course, that isn't the easiest thing to admit, which is probably why is the last conclusion I can come to. Often it is easier to look at the stained-glass window than it is to consider the crystal-clear mirror. I wake up wanting love. Yet I'm lying beside someone that loves me! Wanting children and a family of my own. Yet I can hear the patter of little feet and random yells of "Ma!!" However, that does not equate to flesh of my flesh and blood of my blood. Today I woke up to overdrawn bank accounts, a refrigerator partially stocked mostly with things we buy as space fillers but nothing I readily want. Gas tank almost on "E" and I think to my inner most honest self, the eternal internal me, and I ask "...is this the life or what?" Without trying I am reminded that even what I see is enough to make me grateful. Realizing there is a man under a bridge or a woman and child seeking refuge from the day and elements in a jam-packed car full of their belongings. Immediately I become grateful for the life that I see, I just begin to dig deep and I make a suggestion to God "THERE HAS TO BE MORE TO LIFE…."

There has to be more to life than just existing in the space that you know. What if I just woke up different, rather than just feeling different? Wake up in a space of confidence and security knowing that all I could ever want is just at my fingertips. Its mine for the asking. Its mine for the building. Its very attainable. Do I have to give up all I have now to get it? Is it possible to want so much more and still be content with what already exists? Or does that call for replacing the scenery? How do you

GROW? Flourish? I want the feeling the eagle has once it has kept the momentum and reached the altitude that he gets to rest his wings and soar! Perception is a funny thing, I'm sure there real plausible reasons that a bird "soar". However, from my point of view it seems as if they are taking inventory of all that is before and below. Having immaculate peripheral vision, they can still see portions where they came from but completely aware of what is in front of them. Unapologetically moving in full appreciation.

Is it odd that you can just have an innate feeling to move or go but you have no rhyme or reason to do it other than the urgency that exists only within? No outer influences have the force of GO! I suppose it would seem crazy to hear that is the way the person that holds you tight and breathes with you in the night the same shallow breaths as you; are feeling deep in the core of their being. It wouldn't meet with the logic of reality. It wouldn't make sense. Even now as I complete these thoughts, she is aware that I am "different". She knows I have things that ooze out of me magically and passionately and words are such erotica for me. She allows me this time to sit and be with my thoughts.

She's here but I think in her inner most honest self, she has a burning desire to break free too. It could solely be my conscious making sense of my own feelings and adding her to the equation to make it okay. I understand that it is okay for me to feel however is natural for me. But its not ok for me to not articulate it. The thing about me though, I'm geared more towards logic over emotion. Your emotional self can be wavering. Emotions are fluid. Logic is concrete. You can count on logic to be consistent. As long as the facts are presented, logic can make a strong case for anything that makes common sense. We stay together because we do have a love that has not been shown the way we display it. We mesh well. My strengths show up where her uncertainty resides and vice versa. There is a friendship that has value. Not to mention that *thing* we do. If I long for better days that can be imagined with ME as the leading lady, where does that leave her? Does that X her out? Is it possible for me to consider myself first and it NOT be selfish?

CHAPTER 2

What's the Difference?

How have things changed from the last time I felt "different"? When you come to a crossroad no matter what the choices you make, live your life being real with yourself. There should be no outside influences that can compel you in what the "right direction" may be. That tug should come from within. Learning how to obey that nudge is the rising of adulthood. It is at that point you navigate your own way. You can't just go with the flow. Don't always turn left or right. A leap of faith is saying "...I rather not!" to both directions. I have to create an avenue that allows me to be me, the way I think I should be. Last time I decided to follow the difference of my heart, I ended the longest standing relationship I have had with a man or any human being other than family. To pursue the longing with-in to explore my sexuality with a woman. The act alone is one thing but the accepting it as a lifestyle was something else. All I had to take with me was my faith, the hope that the God of the Heavens will find me in my own lane, the avenue I created. Yes even there!! Fully aware that all

I have ever known to be true is on the line.
All the things I've held in the highest regard
is going to be put to the ultimate test.

My identity has begun reaching
beyond Martha and Chris's daughter. It
surpasses being Jessica and them sister or
even Aisha's girlfriend. My identity as I've
established it to this point is on the line also.
I remember going to college because all the
girls I was close friends with were going or
already enrolled. Not that I had not thought
about continuing my education, but I was
not in a rush. I felt like high school really
took a lot out of me and I wanted some time

to figure out my next steps. I remember feeling as though I would be letting people down if I didn't soon attend. I am not interested in doing the things that "people" think I should be doing. In this next phase of my life, I want to move towards my own aspirations. I have always known mediocrity was not meant for me. I still feel that urgency to be great! Feeling different is tough as hell! There's a longing that can never seem to be filled. I think God allows us to feel this voided area intentionally. This void can go unnoticed as we busy ourselves living as blissfully as we can only imagine. Once you are *still* longer than you intend to be, that stillness become uncomfortable. It is at that place where you can begin to "feel" the void. It sits with you quietly, in the most intrusive way. Only the peculiar feels a void in a life that seems to give you everything.

There are times we have in our possession the things we want but yet there is *still* something missing. When you arrive at this place of acknowledgment more than likely you have created your own lane, you are on a less travelled path than the normal left and right turns. Unchartered territory even. Anytime you are entering into the unknown, you are going to have an experience that is completely out of your realm of expertise. You are inviting life to show you an insight to things the average person may not encounter. There's nothing wrong with being safe or following the expected route, if that's where your individual path leads you and going that way seems organic.

When you have taken losses, faced death, seen your very own life "flash" before your eyes; it is not easy to willingly conform. You should know that no encounter is by happenstance, it is destiny. There are no coincidences in life. Every single thing we see, hear, feel, think and desire has a purpose. I wonder why every time I feel a change in the air, or difference approaching it has a familiar aura. Why as bold as I think I am, I'm afraid to go straight through this next crossroad in my life? I already know I don't want to turn left or right! That's too mediocre to have my name attached to that pathway.

All I know for certain is that I want to remain true to me! Truest to my God first then to myself second, and true to all I may ever encounter. I don't want to forfeit my chance at being "great" by being afraid to admit.... I'm feeling different! I feel more incline to move even beyond my last great change. Does that make this a step backwards? If I'm not satisfied with this beautiful woman does that mean I have to go back in the man-pool? I sure hope not. The pickings are slim on that side too. I think it is healthy to explore all facets of the difference that could come from the power of my decision to pursue another life.

Quite frankly, I am uncertain of where this relationship is going. I know I want children of my own. I show up in the world fully a woman with resting masculine energy but I would absolutely house my own fetus. I would endure what women have endured since the beginning of time to bring forth life. In the lesbian lifestyle, it is still a little taboo for the dominant figure to carry especially if the dominance is expressed with masculine energy attached. However, time moves forward without notice or consent. I too want to move like time…without notice and consent!!! Free to be me! I JUST WANT TO FEEL LIBERATED!

This life that I created for myself is starting to suffocate me. Something is not being fulfilled. I often allow myself to envision a version of me that is MORE than a worker. She's the boss. She signs the checks and disperse them. That woman is strong and vulnerable but never weak. Assertive but not down-trotting. Well known and accomplished. Approachable yet very reserved.

I think I spent too much time growing with the people that I love. I think this time around, I want to find the depth that comes from growing alone. At my own pace. Every win belongs to me and every lesson from a loss I will bear the sole responsibility for because the decision was all mine. I think that is how you are suppose to grow. Life will give you all the conditions; sunshine and rain. I don't have a plan. Other than the motto that governs my life "To thine own-self be true, first and always"!

Another difference I can see, I have an outlet for all the things I may feel this time around. When I began my journey loving a woman, she was the only person I could talk about the feelings and experiences I was having. For a full year, I uttered not a word of our secret rendezvous or overly passionate disagreements. I did write then, but it was always just to her! She has read a lot of the things I experienced emotionally during our secret courtship but there is still plenty that would be fresh to her eyes. We have been living openly for years and its pretty much accepted as a norm for her friends and mine.

CHAPTER 3

Life After

I have expectations, but no demands. I expect liberation. The freedom to be true to God and anyone that cross my path. I expect to move beyond mediocrity. I expect to propel myself into my destiny; knowing the God has already equipped me with all the knowledge, vision and experience to enhance my own life and perhaps someone else life as well. I expect to be diagnosed as fraudulent in a world full of frauds. I'm ok with being misunderstood. I'm ok with being made fun of. If every opinion of me is based on a real fact, it's more than OK. I have no idea what the future holds.

If I could go back to that hazy night in April or to the morning after, where the linger of inebriation coupled with the stench of lust met me in the doorway of her bedroom, I would still take every step toward her all over again. I would still pause the way I did, relishing in the moment of desire. As we sat on the cusp of no-return, fully aware that if I did what she wanted, we would be forever different! I would take that chance all over again! There are definitely growing pains I wish she did not have to experience. If I could change anything, I would redo those moments of ego-driven decisions. Those times I was testing myself knowing I would fail.

When I started, I already knew that difference would come for me one day. I suppose I was meant to engage but perhaps it doesn't mean you will always stay in the same realm of difference. Variety is the spice of life, or so they say. Perhaps difference and feeling different is a constant and consistent part of growth and development. No one is designed to remain the same forever. The problem is we attempt to box people in. We get stuck on the preconceived notions of who they are at one season in time. Then we ostracize, even the ones we love the most for feeling unlike most when no one is excluded or immune to having a different outlook on life or themselves.

The direction your life takes is a combination of desires and fears. You can't be afraid to live the life you want. The life that makes you happy. When you have reached your crossroad and no matter which direction you head in...everything that lies in that path is for you. Be it good or bad. Amazing or terrible. It's yours. Own it.

Life will present you another crossroad, and if you feel the same you may continue the road you are travelling. However, if you are ready to know what the other avenues have in store, because no two paths have the same outcome, take a chance on yourself. Make a decision that may not please the masses but will give you useful nuggets of truth. Life is filled with so many choices. When you really understand the value that comes from the power of a decision, THAT is the fullness of being free and completely liberated.

To free yourself from the opinions of people. So many people won't dare follow their heart because of how that decision may or may not affect someone else. How life will be after I make a decision, I can just hope I reach that place of self-actualization. That moment of clarity where I can piece together the fragments and pinpoint the beginning of everything. I want it to all make sense. Otherwise, I will probably ruin the best relationship I have experienced so far in my adult life. What I gain in my latter days will be worth all I am willing to give up in my present.

Freedom comes not without cost. Its going to cost me something. The life I envision isn't cheap and it doesn't just happen. Trial and error but most importantly, effort without fear is required. Ultimately, I expect to be more sensitive and understanding to other people wanting difference. I want to genuinely allow people to change their lives and make decisions based on what feels organic to them. I don't want to be a hypocrite when it comes to someone feeling different. It's laughable to expect someone to accept all the ways I feel if I refuse to give the same level of understanding to changes that may go against an idea I once held as a certainty. Everyone goes through changes. There are periods in life where it is very possible to have the vision revised without your consent. It gets uncomfortable for everyone involved. The scary part is that it can happen at any time to anyone

~C'est La Vie

CHAPTER 4

The Faith

I think I may have had faith for as long as I've had my breast. Young and flat chested I interlocked my fingers together elbows raised near my chest and I began to flap my arms as wings chanting "I must, I must, I must increase my bust"! Why? I have no idea. I suppose I was feeling different then also. A little girl but not girly enough perhaps. Being raised in a religious/spiritual family was God's greatest gift to me. I've always gone to church. A place of worship. Whether it be the humble beginnings of store front sanctuaries and summer tent revivals or the swelling buzz of worship in the mega churches with jumbotron screens displaying large mass choirs. In those times, My God mother Carrie would hold a bible study in her living room every Saturday people from all over would come. As a child I remember us being a little on the poor side for a while. Thus, I spent a lot of time with Carrie. When 8pm came I would have to go in the living room and sit in on the class.

There would be assignments that had to be read before the next session. Questionnaires that required researching scripture.

I was the youngest in the 1994 evangelistic course in Staten Island, NY. Looking back, who knew what an impact that would have on me. The things I would retain from that year and a half. I think at the time I really wanted to appease my Godmother. Afterall, she had often gone out her way for me. Carrie was always so impressed with all that I could retain and recite verbatim.

Faith to me is simply belief in hopes. The hope of my world is in God. Biblically referred to the God of Abraham, Isaac and Jacob. I believe He wants what is best for me, often He will allow me to have amazing things. The best life has to offer. Even if I don't ask for it or even believe that I deserve it. One story I don't tell often yet it is very true. My faith was solid until a great adversarial energy began to attack me in my most intimate space, my mind. November 30th, 2008 my mother died. She breathed her last breath while two of my sisters, my mom's only sister, a then friend of the family and myself watched helplessly.

Because I was the chosen one for the past two days during her hospitalization to say the words of prayer, I prayed. For some reason the way I chose to pray was more so offering thanksgiving to God for the caliber of woman he chose to bring us into this world. Never really making a request for restoration. When she passed away. A few weeks after the funeral I mourned but I won't say I grieved properly. I constantly had to have a potent potion of liquors, pills, and marijuana. All day, every day. I survived financially from the life insurance policy my mother left.

One day while I allowed myself to wallow in my despair I was suddenly vexed with a high level of guilt. A guilt that I couldn't deny held truth factors. I was led to believe that because of my relationship, albeit active and true, relationship with God I could have asked for anything from him in those moments of prayer and by faith God would have brought it to pass. The fact that I never specifically (because I believe you must be clear and deliberate in your words when you make a request to God) asked for God to heal her, restore her fully and give her a testimony of His power that was the reason she was dead! And I thanked Him as she laid there dying…I felt maybe I didn't earnestly pray for her the right way.

Ultimately it was my fault. It was my fault she was gone. I'm the reason my sisters and I are motherless children. Our kids will live life without the love of a maternal grandmother. Even caused my father to lose all chances of restoring his marriage, the great love of his life with his only wife! Honestly, I still believe if I would have made a request God would have honored it. Not because I'm that good, undefiled, or untarnished of a saint. It's just that I am familiar with His power. I believe whole heartedly in His existence, His capability

and love for me as His creation. That

adverse mental attack draped in guilt could

have destroyed me mentally and ruined all

future hope. Instead it had the direct effect

of the future prayer request. I ask boldly for

strange undeserved things because God is

God! He is moved by our faith. He is

inclined to hear us when in our hearts, mind,

soul, and mouth believe he can and that he

will. Blind faith goes a step further and say

even if God doesn't give me what I request,

I know without a doubt that He is able. His

denial of one request is only because he

already has it worked out for us in a way we haven't thought of yet.

I think the biggest hope in my heart is that I'm not a broken woman, and I CAN bare children. I no longer sleep with men, but I hope that my body can accept sperm properly positioned and can nurture life. I have never been pregnant. I have had lengthy relations that never produced fruit. The one time my cycle disappeared for too long, I was in college. I was having relations with an athlete on campus and I remember praying to God "Not him!! Of all the people in the world, NOT HIM!" Very clear I heard the phrase "Your mother won't live to see your kids." Immediately I began to shun the thought. Questioning why of all the things to utter in my inner parts, why that? Its with faith and the passing of time I can say with certainty, my mother died. She did not live to see my kids. Hell, at this rate, I haven't lived to see my kids either. But I heard it. So, I hold fast to the hope that its in the cards. How will I conceive when I do not willfully or otherwise engage in sexual intercourse with men? I have not figured that part out yet.

I also have deep faith in the greatest love of my life. If indeed I do not have that love now, I believe it must find me or I must find it! Our worlds absolutely must collide. I have to live in that space of complete happiness with another person unapologetically showing up in the world their bold and beautiful self. I want to appreciate our differences. I want to be challenged and compelled to forever dig beyond the façade. To uncover and respect the independence of their individuality. Fully secure and confident that every fiber of energy I invest into the building of us is equally met with tenacity and compassion.

Selfishly and selflessly loving another person. Withholding no good thing from them. Experience every wonder earth has to offer with my best friend at my side. Sharing life, love and legacy with one person until death causes us to part. Cliché'? Maybe. I rather be cliché over cynical any day.

CHAPTER 5

Homosexuality….as it relates

to me

I'm 30 years old. Unwed. No

children. Black female actively in a lesbian

relationship. I once asked God if loving

Aisha was wrong? I would like to think that

I have a decent relationship, to say the least

with the Most High. We dialogue frequently. I'm not estranged from His presence. I still consult Him for most of what I do. As for the parts I don't seek His guidance I already know what he thinks in those situations. Religion shows up in many areas in my life because I have been conditioned to incorporate it in everything. And so, I do.

I've loved a woman and lusted a few others. Yet my question "is loving a woman wrong?" has gone unanswered to this day. I have not heard a definitive yes or no! So, I draw the conclusion God is love. Anytime unconditional endearment really exists, it is not wrong. *How* to love may be a different story. I once asked God to "Show me, me" I began to feel as though an external force had attacked me from all sides as often as possible. It feels as though, there is some tidbit of information about my latter days that has eluded being revealed to me. However, it is visible to that external force, the sole purpose for it being active and present is to deter and to distract me from pressing toward all that is destined for me. To keep me complacent so that I do not reach that place that has been afforded to me at a later day. One decision in the right direction after another will put me on a direct path to greatness. Yet I am distracted and knocked out of my own race.

Because I was raised with religious background, one would perceive that my lifestyle prevents me from reaching destiny. All I know is God allows the sun to shine and the rain to fall on the just and the unjust. So that can't be it. Besides, if God really is all knowing, didn't He know I would get here at some point. Seems like a condescending God to purposely punish me entering a space He saw coming way before I did. Knowing I love love. I crave attention and long for loving affections. I suppose the men I've encountered prior to my

exploration of my own sexuality had not

fulfilled those gaping holes within.

Scared to admit that I was even

having thoughts and fantasies the included

women. Seeing beauty in women really

changed me. So naturally I was face to face

with a dilemma. Trying to make sense if

why I'm feeling this way. I began to wonder

if indeed God created me to have these

feelings. Was I born already with the desire

for women. Although, contrary to popular

belief I had never been sexually attracted to

other women before I encounter Esha!

People often ask about my opinion on the subject "born gay or decided to be gay" Quite frankly I believe it's a little of both. Under the pretense that we are born into a "world of sin", you have the propensity to complete any behavior that is deemed undesirable or unacceptable. However, we are self-aware when one makes the choice to act without provocation. The moment when you give in completely to an inner desire, that is the choice. A decision is made when you opt out of dating the opposite sex all together. Even if you are following a natural feeling. That does not negate the free-will aspect. There is the accepted norm. Just like there is what feels more organic to an individual and you choose to be ok with what you feel.

Homosexuality isn't biological. It's not hereditary. I was born a female. I was born with dark skin, of African descent. Unarguably facets I had no say so in. I choose my life. I did not ask to be aroused by some soap on the corner of her back that time she came out in a towel before the club. However, I chose to notice if it was a trend, that she doesn't turn fully on that last rinse before she gets out the shower. I chose to express partially the thoughts I was having about her. She chose to remember that conversation and she chose to treat me especially different after that conversation. I chose a lot of avenues that led up to that crossroad. That do or die moment. When that moment came…we fully participated. When feelings grew, we acknowledged and I chose to ask her "be gay with me..." she chose to accompany me on the first part of my journey.

How an individual is introduced to homosexuality varies. I have no quarrels with anything that has brought anyone to their particular journey. Yet it's one thing we all have in common. That is the first pursuit. Full of free will. A carefully considered decision.

A child lying in a nursery is pure, clean and undefiled. It's the exposure to the world and all the contaminates and all the choices that help mold and penetrates the heart that help to dictate the decisions. It's the duality that exist in the earth. For every opportunity, there is to do what is considered right, the same opportunity to do the opposite is also very present.

I can't speak for everyone when it comes to the subject and lifestyle of homosexuality, but I can say with a surety and certainty that EVERYONE that actively chooses to live freely in their desires and date within the same sex realm, regardless to how it was presented as an option "A CONSCIOUS CHOICE" was made when the individual decided to pursue on their own accord, without any prompting or baiting. Whether from day one it was a desire, I think that is something that varies from person to person. But for everyone that made attempts to date in the "norm of life" then decided to stop being conventional.... made a choice!

CHAPTER 6

The Hope

When I began writing my thoughts and feelings, I didn't realize how naked I had to become. After realizing the vulnerability and soul bearing honesty it takes to complete this project, I hope anyone who encounters this be it in whole or in part, examines their own truth and take up residence right there!

I hope this bare honesty is pleasing God, because He knows better than anyone how real this content is. I swear my point of view and opinion is all I have that will forever be mine. We are overcomers through our testimony. No, I didn't intend to "testify" or anything too religious. However, I did purposely intend to share the makings of me. I hope that all these different feelings aren't for nothing. I hope that any bonds that break because of these feelings can be restored after understanding has taken a seat at the table. I hope to not break the spirits of them that I have cared for on my journey of self-discovery.

Right now, I am currently unemployed. I can barely pay my bills. I am a regular, run of the mill yet extraordinary amazingly different kind of woman. I hope my absolute best days are ahead of me. I hope I can find a peaceful way to live in my truth. I hope to one day be called "mom". I think *THAT* is the complete joy that comes with being a woman. Women that enter a lesbian relationship after having children will not be able to identify with that hope, but just take a moment to look at your children. Admire their beauty that looks familiar to you. Acknowledge for a moment their personality that is strikingly like your own. The absence of my own causes me to dote heavily on other children.

I hope to one day be a wife! I have always said "Happy wife, happy life!" To marry a woman, may she never forget that I too am a wife! I want no parts of titles that take away from my birth right as a woman. Part of living a purpose filled life is being OK with being vulnerable. Vulnerable enough to expose your truth, to let that uncertainty within be seen. Yet still secure and together enough to be proud of yourself. I share the issues of my heart not because I enjoy telling all my personal short comings but so that someone else will know "It's OK, you are not alone". There's no guide book to everything that will happen. The Bible is great and by no means to I intend to belittle it. However, there is no "HOW TO GUIDE" or how to go through life on the shelves of Barnes and Noble. Therefore, I hope that we can become more intuitive and listen to our higher selves and know when it's time to expose the contents of your soul. It is in that bare skin we are liberated to be our true perfectly imperfect divinely driven self.

CHAPTER 7

The Liberation

I've never wanted freedom so bad.

Freedom from almost everything. Free from

lack. Free from poverty. Free from violence

that surrounding me that also traumatize so

many of my friends and loved ones.

Freedom from worldly intoxications. Sighs.

That is a secret shame and an absolution in

my world. Its 2016, 10 years ago, the only

"drug" I was familiar with was marijuana.
Fast forward and at least $150,000 later I
know, marijuana, ecstasy, molly,
oxycodone, hydrocodone all with elixirs of
Hennessy and Four Lokos, Black and mild's
and Newport's. Keep my brain and lungs so
clouded. It's always a struggle to catch my
breath.

I'm in a loving relationship that the
insane part of me wants out of sometimes
because I feel unfulfilled as a woman. I
don't necessarily desire a man. For me, it
was never about attraction. I choose to not
date them anymore. But I do want to be

open to whatever God has for me. It's my belief that my life in this earthly realm was all configured before 3:06pm on July 14, 1986. The creator of life had already mapped out my paths and knowing mc before I knew myself, He knew I would get to this point. He knew I would want to write about it. But He also knew I would procrastinate out of fear, uncertainty and slight shame even. As I stated before as I write now, I am currently unemployed, due to self-sabotage. I want so desperately to be freed from that too…the ability to disturb and disrupt even the most positive things I have going for myself, by tricking myself into believing I don't deserve it. ME not having all I need or all that I have become accustomed to is my fault. We must stop looking at external factors and focus more on the self-inflicted sores. This thorn in my side, ultimately, I placed it there. I also want to be freed from condemnation.

Condemnation can come from internal and external sources. We know it to be "kicking ourselves" but in fact the first time we acknowledge our better options that was available is sufficient. That point you KEEP kicking yourself or at any given moment is reminded of how your current dilemma is your fault, you are condemning yourself. STOP IT! For there is now NO CONDEMNATION if any man be in Christ, He is a new creature. So, as I write this I am made anew. I want liberation for all those who want it for themselves. Growing up is a constant thing. Even when you have reached adulthood, you encounter new situations, different hardships that will pull, push and pry all kinds of things in and out of you. Ever just look at the television and wonder how those celebrities lived prior to their "big break"? They were someone who had all the responsibilities of someone relying on them but they didn't have the answers. They were just like you and me. However, THEY FELT DIFFERENT! They too wanted to be liberated. Free to be free. Free to live, to love, to provide effortlessly, free to give, and free to have something more in life. Free to be at peace. I want the freedom to dream big on purpose. I want a life that does not need validation. I try to exude that kind of force now, however, I don't think I have mastered it. I do still strive to attain it. I want to be me, without due rhyme or reason. I don't want to have to constantly give disclaimers to the people who claim to know me and love me as I am. I feel different. And I am okay with that!

Feeling Different

Feeling Different

Made in the USA
Columbia, SC
02 June 2020

97659702R00040